W9-AEE-064

CONTEMPORARY MUSICIANS
AND THEIR MUSIC™

Christina Aguilera

Robert Greenberger

ROSEN
PUBLISHING

New York

Dedicated to Kate, who has always shared her musical passions with me

Published in 2009 by The Rosen Publishing Group, Inc.
29 East 21st Street, New York, NY 10010

First Edition

Library of Congress Cataloging-in-Publication Data

Greenberger, Robert.
Christina Aguilera / Robert Greenberger.—1st ed.
   p. cm.—(Contemporary musicians and their music)
Includes discography (p. 42), bibliographical references (p. 46) and index.
ISBN-13: 978-1-4042-1816-1 (library binding)
ISBN-13: 978-1-4358-5124-5 (pbk)
ISBN-13: 978-1-4042-7869-1 (6 pack)
1. Aguilera, Christina, 1980—Juvenile literature. 2. Singers—United States—Juvenile literature. I. Title.
ML3930.A36G76 2009
782.42164092—dc22

                                                              2007051058

Manufactured in Malaysia

On the cover: Christina Aguilera performs before a crowd of adoring fans.

Contents

Introduction

In the latter half of the twentieth century, many celebrities blurred the line between being talented and just being famous. Some celebrities had talent as well as fame. Others were just famous, but both gained attention from a growing number of outlets devoted to the comings and goings of the celebrities. This phenomenon began with weekly tabloids and magazines, and it exploded with the growth of celebrity coverage on cable television and then on the Internet. As a result, the very notion of talent was sometimes lost amidst the

Christina Aguilera, a showstopper in any arena, performs at the February 2007 NBA All-Star Game.

harsh glare of the spotlight, and people may have forgotten why someone ever got attention to begin with.

Christina Aguilera was noticed because she could truly sing. Many critics have acknowledged that her voice is indeed powerful and compelling. When Aguilera sings, her voice displays a range that most of her peers envy. She was never formerly trained, and yet she managed to rise head and shoulders above her contemporaries from an early age. Thanks to influences at home, both good and bad, Aguilera was able to draw inspiration from older styles of music that she fused into her own works.

Christina Aguilera was the right girl in the right place at the right time, since in the 1990s talented people were provided with vehicles that didn't previously exist. She first gained attention as a member of an ensemble television program that featured simplistic musical numbers geared toward children. Her vast vocal range surprised many, and it has been on display on album after album. Aguilera's style has spanned songs reflecting her Latin American heritage to duets with legendary crooner Tony Bennett.

Along the way, she has challenged herself as a singer, song-writer, and performer by constantly reinventing her onstage persona to avoid being typecast by those in the recording industry and in the media. Some of it worked, as noted by her awards and album sales. But some of it brought her harsh attention as she strained the boundaries of what was considered decent.

Her albums have sold millions of copies around the world, and her constantly changing public persona has allowed her the freedom to express herself in new ways, providing her audience with material that they could not hear elsewhere.

Aguilera's popularity is such that she has half a million friends on her MySpace page and her every move is chronicled by the press. There is little doubt that she has the talent and ability to remain a force in the music world for years to come.

She has used her celebrity status to speak out on a variety of issues close to her heart, but she has also had to deal with unwanted attention because of her fame. During the fall of 2007, the speculation over her unannounced pregnancy fueled the media for weeks. But as usual, Aguilera seized control of the situation. When it was time to announce her pregnancy, she did so in a provocative cover story in the January 2008 issue of *Marie Claire*, a magazine not necessarily aimed at her core audience of teen girls.

What follows explores the experiences that forged Christina Aguilera into a vocal powerhouse.

Chapter One

From Talent Contestant to Pop Star

Christina Maria Aguilera was born on December 18, 1980, in Staten Island, New York. She was the child of Fausto Wagner Xavier Aguilera, who was Ecuadorian, and Shelly Loraine Fidler, who was Irish American. Fausto was also a sergeant in the U.S. Army. His career required him to move his family around the world, including postings in Canada and Japan, before returning to the United States.

Christina Aguilera's early childhood was filled with not only frequent relocation but also physical and emotional abuse from her angry father. By the time Christina was seven years old, her parents had decided to divorce. Shelly moved, taking Christina and her sister, Rachel, to live with her mother, Delcie Fidler, in the Pittsburgh, Pennsylvania, suburb of Rochester. Christina had taken to singing and performing, displaying an amazing gift that people immediately recognized as one that could make her a star. Looking back, she realized that she began using her talent to avoid her father's frequent abuse.

"My grandma was the first to realize that singing was something I did all the time," she told *Rolling Stone*. "[It was] something I loved. For me, my voice and music [were] always an outlet. Growing up in an unstable environment and whatnot, music was my only real escape."

Discovering Her Talent

While Christina was in elementary school, others discovered her singing ability when she performed in talent shows. Her skill, at age six, was clearly beyond her peers, and she suffered their jealously. This made her childhood more difficult.

Jude Pohl, host of Pittsburgh's *Jude Pohl's Talent Showcase*, told VH1, "It was almost not fair to send anybody against her. It was like sending the lamb to the slaughter." As a result, if Christina signed up for a talent show, others would almost immediately drop out. "I knew she wasn't just your average nine-year-old," said Noelle Bannister, who competed against Christina at the time.

In fact, as time passed, people turned their jealousy into physical acts of aggression, such as threats and slashing the tires of the Aguilera family car. Eventually, Christina's family had to leave Rochester. One of her few friends, Katie Heffner, recalled, "She had a lot of self-confidence, which sometimes can be mistaken for arrogance."

The Mickey Mouse Club

Christina's big break finally arrived when she was invited to join the cast of *The All New Mickey Mouse Club* for its last two seasons on cable TV's Disney Channel. The twelve-year-old loved singing

and performing, and it turned out that she was one of many cast members who would make a splash in the entertainment world. The experience on the cable program also convinced

This promotional photo shows the cast of *The All New Mickey Mouse Club*, which proved to be a launching pad for many young talents.

the young teen that she wanted to release an album prior to her high school graduation.

The All New Mickey Mouse Club was a revival of the original television series from the 1950s that turned regular adolescents into performers. While several of the original cast members, like Annette Funnicello, went on to greater fame, no set of members would achieve the kind of fame and fortune that the cast from the final two seasons of the revived program achieved. From 1993 to 1995, the cast of *The All New Mickey Mouse Club* included Christina Aguilera, Britney Spears, Justin Timberlake, Ryan Gosling, Rhona Bennett, Keri Russell, and JC Chasez.

On VH1's documentary show *Driven*, Matt Casella, the show's casting director said, "They'd call her the diva. They all sort of took a step back and went, 'Oh boy, I'm gonna lose a few solo songs this season.'"

Thus began Disney's careful casting, grooming, and promoting of actors and singers for its subsequent television series and telefilms. The culmination of these efforts was *High School Musical*, the Disney Channel's original movie that became an international phenomenon. It also became a template emulated by rival cable channel Nickelodeon, with both channels manufacturing bubblegum pop stars with regularity.

As the Disney series wound down in 1995, Christina used it as a stepping stone, traveling from Los Angeles to Japan, where she recorded "All I Wanna Do" with Keizo Nakanishi. Nakanishi was Japan's reigning pop star at the time. The experience was a successful one, and she returned to the United States and made plans to record demos (demonstration songs for record companies). Her most famous demo was recorded in her own bathroom, where she achieved a high E above middle C note that caught people's attention. Christina's skill coupled with her familiarity with the Walt Disney Company led to her being signed to sing "Reflection" for the soundtrack to Disney's 1998 animated film *Mulan*. Around the same time, she landed her first recording contract, with RCA records.

The animated film opened to positive reviews. It pulled in

Mulan was one of a long string of successful films from Disney that showcased new talent, including Christina Aguilera, who contributed to the soundtrack.

sterling box-office receipts in June 1998. "Reflection" made the Top 15 on the Adult Contemporary music charts. In support of the single, Christina sang the number on both *CBS This Morning* and the *Donnie & Marie* talk show. The song would later earn her a Golden Globe nomination for Best Original Song in a Motion Picture.

Making Her Mark

Christina's talent took her far beyond television shows. Over the next few years, she remained in Pittsburgh and sang the national anthem at the games of the city's sports teams, the Penguins, the Pirates, and the Steelers. It was as if Christina were biding her time until the right opportunity presented itself to her.

During this time, she found herself being mentored by Walt

Aguilera, even from an early age, belted out her songs with a flair for the dramatic.

Pop Stars Through the Years

As popular music grew into a national craze in the 1940s, various young singers became recognized as celebrities at earlier and earlier ages. This mania reached fever pitch during the 1950s, when Elvis Presley became a sensation followed by Frankie Avalon and Fabian. Teen stars from television and films were encouraged to record singles, and many of these stars gained new fans through their songs. Among them was Ricky Nelson, who was featured on television program *The Adventures of Ozzie and Harriet.* In the 1960s, two groups of singing brothers hit the music charts, but the youngest member of both broke out as solo acts competing with one another to amass number-one hits. Michael Jackson and Donny Osmond continued to entertain well into adulthood.

The 1980s and 1990s saw an increase of younger stars. This included country sensation LeAnn Rimes, who had her first hit when she was just thirteen years old.

The growth of cable music channels, beginning with MTV, provided new showcases for these child singers to be discovered on a wider scale. Talent agents went out and created bands such as Menudo, 98 Degrees, and the Backstreet Boys in order to capitalize on the hunger for new sounds and franchises to promote. All had music videos receiving heavy rotation on the channel, and their tours proved to be big successes. But their album sales were the true measure of the tastemakers' skills as each set new records.

Maddox. Maddox had performed during the 1960s as a member of the Marcels, a doo-wop band. He told VH1, "Once you saw Christina and heard Christina, there was just no way you could ever forget the voice of this little kid."

Moving Up

By the age of seventeen, Christina Aguilera was ready to become a recording artist. She packed her bags to permanently relocate to Los Angeles, California. She left Pittsburgh behind; she wasn't going to miss the unrelenting misery from her peers. During Christina's high school prom, the DJ played her single, "Genie in a Bottle," and the dance floor cleared.

Chapter Two

Finding Her Style

Upon signing Christina Aguilera, Bob Jamieson, president of RCA Records, said, "She's a strong woman. And she has opinions and she'll express those opinions. This is not a woman that's going to sit in a corner and do what people tell her to do."

Aguilera later told *Time* magazine, "As soon as I came to the point where we were going to release my album, the label was like, you know, 'This name, it's too difficult to pronounce.' They wanted it to be more American sounding. I said no because this is my name. It's my identity."

The album, *Christina Aguilera*, had a variety of songwriters and producers handling the tracks, and each of them tried to take Aguilera's voice and turn it into something people of all ages wanted to buy. Guy Roche produced her single "What a Girl

Christina Aguilera has become a music awards fixture since her debut. Here, she is seen singing at the 27th American Music Awards show in 2000.

Wants," while David Frank and Steve Kipner took control of "Genie in a Bottle." Later, she told Sing365.com that she was proudest of the album's ballads, not the pop classics. The ballads strongly reflected the influence that past singers had on Aguilera.

"Genie in a Bottle"

"Genie in a Bottle" was the first single, and it hit number one on the pop charts for five consecutive weeks. This propelled the following album to the top of the charts when it arrived in August 1999. Her second single from the record, "What a Girl Wants," was the first Billboard Hot 100 number one for the year 2000. The album went on to sell at multiple-platinum levels, meaning that millions of copies were purchased in the United States.

As her fame grew, Aguilera continued to reinvent her look for a ravenous press corps. She dyed her hair and changed her clothing style with startling regularity.

People noticed this new star, and *Ladies' Home Journal* named her one of 1999's most fascinating women. She was also recognized as Best New Artist at the ALMA Awards, an event honoring the top Hispanic American performers.

Pop Princesses

Since pop music became a distinct music category back in the 1960s, it has had its share of reigning kings and queens. In recent years, women seem to have garnered the most attention, led by singers such as Christina Aguilera and Britney Spears, who were once friends but became rivals.

In October 2007, Gainesville State College's paper, *The Voice*, opined, "You remember them. As much as we may hate to admit it, we all remember them. Whether it was the parachute pants, the infamous haircuts, or the 'innocent' acts they played, you remember them. They were the pop stars of the late '90s. They were on top of the world; they had power, fame, and tons of fans. The boy bands and pop princesses we once loved don't rule the radio anymore. Some of these pop stars have kept a steady path to the top and some have hit rock bottom." As a result, the attention they have received is more about their antics away from the recording studio than their actual performing.

With her first album, Christina Aguilera earned two Grammy Award nominations and, in February 2000, she was named Best New Artist. "It was an incredible shock for me," she told Sing365.com. "I was completely unprepared. My album had been out the least amount of time compared to everyone else, so I thought there was no way I'd win. But I was overwhelmed, shocked, and overjoyed all at the same time." With her beautiful image, she was a hot commodity for magazine covers, ranging from *Teen People* to *Entertainment Weekly*.

Embracing Her Latin Heritage

When her debut album arrived in 1999, Christina Aguilera was one of several Latin American

Aguilera and Ricky Martin performed together at the 2001 World Music Awards. The two toured together for forty-five performances.

20

performers to suddenly come into vogue. She was accompanied by Ricky Martin, Jennifer Lopez, and the South American sensation Shakira.

Aguilera's second album was *Mi Reflejo*. It featured Spanish-language versions of tracks from her first release and other songs that were selected for the somewhat different audience. The September 12, 2000, release did well enough in America to reach the Billboard 200's twenty-seventh spot, and it went on to sell 2.5 million copies around the world. She was awarded the Best Female Pop Vocal Album at the 2001 Latin Grammy Award ceremony. She then won the World Music Award's citation for being the best-selling Latin artist that year.

In interviews, Aguilera never shied away from discussing her heritage and told *Time* magazine, "I think because I went to a pretty white school, that I really don't look Latin. I don't have dark eyes. I never had dark hair. So, I don't think a lot of people put two and two together. But I was always proud of my Latino roots and proud of my Irish roots. I never felt like, 'Oh, I should be white, or all Latin.' I am what I am."

She was asked to sing with Ricky Martin on "Nobody Wants to Be Lonely," which appeared on Martin's 2001 album, *Sound Loaded*. When Aguilera was pregnant in 2007, she told *InStyle* magazine, "I definitely want my kids to know Spanish. And I'm taking my tapes on tour."

Her New Album

Aguilera promoted *Mi Reflejo* by appearing on numerous television shows including *Saturday Night Live*. She also was exposed to older audiences by singing "The Christmas Song" before President Clinton for the annual *Christmas at the White House* television special. Clinton was so impressed by her talent that he asked her to be part of the Millennium Special coming from Washington. She actually had to turn the president down given her commitment to sing in New York City for MTV's New Year's Eve special.

A month later, she sang a duet with Enrique Iglesias as part of the Super Bowl's highly watched halftime show. This appearance further established Aguilera in the minds of people of all ages. She was at the forefront of a series of new singing sensations that included her fellow Mickey Mouse Club member Britney Spears. They, along with Mandy Moore and Willa Ford, were dubbed the "pop princesses" by the media.

Aguilera's singles appealed to generally the same audience, mainly adolescent girls. However, her other appearances demonstrated a greater vocal range and song selection, which put her

Enrique Iglesias and Christina Aguilera sang during the halftime show of Super Bowl XXXIV. Her fame was clearly growing.

career on a different track than that of her contemporaries. She proved that with her second album, *Mi Reflejo*, which was aimed at the Latin audience and her third release, *My Kind of Christmas*, which was marketed to a broader range of consumers. The October 24, 2000, release reached number twenty-eight on the Billboard 200. It went on to sell 1.5 million copies worldwide.

Chapter Three

A Maturing Career

With great fame also came turbulent times for Christina Aguilera. In July 2000, Ruth G. Inniss, who first represented the singer when she was still a twelve-year-old Mouseketeer, sued Aguilera's mother and her second manager, Steve E. Kurtz, for breaking their agreement.

In October, Aguilera switched management again, abandoning Kurtz, who represented her for the previous three years. She then sued Kurtz, claiming in legal papers that he exerted "undue influence" over her personal and professional lives. He counter-sued, and his filing indicated that the nineteen-year-old had already earned $15 million since their legal partnership began.

As the cases wound up in the courts, without resolution, Aguilera concentrated on her career. She was invited to join Lil'

From left to right: Pink, Mya, Lil' Kim, and Christina Aguilera present the Best Male Video Award at the MTV Video Music Awards in New York.

Kim, Mya, and Pink in recording a cover version of LaBelle's 1975 hit single "Lady Marmalade" for the *Moulin Rouge!* soundtrack.

The new single was number one on the Billboard Hot 100 chart for five straight weeks. It also earned the quartet Best Pop Collaboration with Vocals at the Grammy Awards. The single's music video was named MTV's Video of the Year in 2001.

Aguilera once more got involved in a legal tangle when Warlock Records wanted to release an album, *Just Be Free*, using the demo tracks she had recorded when she was fourteen years old. The record company teased the public by releasing the title track as a single, prompting RCA to tell her fans to avoid purchasing it and Aguilera to sue. They settled before matters went to trial, and Warlock Records was allowed to release the album. Aguilera received an undisclosed sum of money from the deal. *Just Be Free* was finally released in August 2001, but it generated minimal interest.

Protecting Her Career

Preferring to seize control of her career once and for all, Aguilera switched from Steve E. Kurtz to industry veteran Irving Azoff as her manager. She wanted to write some of her own material, and she used the process to get rid of the pain she had endured when she felt betrayed by friends, family, and management as she went from newcomer to major international celebrity. She told Britain's Sky News that she had a nervous breakdown in April 2002. "This record saved me from insanity," Aguilera said of her second major release. "A couple of very close people to me who I confided in have sold me out for money—confidantes who were working for me and who I trusted. It's sad learning in this business that money is more important to people than friendship."

Musical Influences

Who was Christina Aguilera and what music did she want to make? Her musical influences ranged from the big-voiced singers from decades past, such as Etta James, to later performers, such as Guns 'N Roses.

From the beginning, Aguilera was singing songs that were initially made popular by pop stars of earlier eras: Billie Holiday, Otis Redding, Ella Fitzgerald, and Pearl Bailey. Her grandmother often took Aguilera to Pittsburgh, Pennsylvania, where the two sought out soul and blues albums. A fast study, Aguilera would have most of the songs memorized and ready to sing within days.

Aguilera's influences include Billie Holiday, a major singer from the 1940s and 1950s.

Her talent-show performances and later recorded music showcased her influences from rhythm and blues, Latin pop, jazz, dance pop, and rock and roll. She initially felt shoehorned into using only her pop side for her debut album. She then explored her Latin heritage for her second release. It wasn't until her album *Stripped* that Aguilera got to display her real range.

She took her painful personal experiences, melded them with the music she grew up loving, and wound up cowriting most of the music on that album.

Aguilera's next album, *Stripped*, was going to display her musical roots and her range, rather than RCA's push into merely the pop category. "The whole vision for this record was to be really raw and real," she told the *New York Times* prior to the album's October 2002 release. "Just really baring who I really am." She cowrote most of the music on *Stripped* and handpicked the producers.

Putting on a more provocative persona, she went on tour in support of *Stripped*. Her music video for the album's first single, "Dirrty," ended up being highly controversial. The video brought her tremendous criticism for the image she portrayed to her younger fans. She suddenly went from innocent pop star to bad girl, a designation that continued to haunt her for years.

As a result of Aguilera's new much-photographed, bad-girl image, people didn't focus as much on the music itself, despite the universally positive notices it received from critics worldwide. The album stalled at number two on the sales charts, and "Dirrty" was a bigger hit overseas than at home. *Stripped*'s second single, "Beautiful," received greater airplay and brought Aguilera a Grammy Award for Best Female Pop Vocal Performance. Three additional singles followed over the next two years while she continued to perform solo concerts. She also joined fellow former

Christina Aguilera performs a song in concert from her album *Stripped* at Staples Center in Los Angeles, California.

Mouseketeer Justin Timberlake in June 2003 for forty-five dates on his concert tour.

That fall, Aguilera continued her *Stripped* tour solo, and *Rolling Stone* readers named it the best concert of the year. Her international fame was sealed when she was asked to host MTV Europe's Music Video Awards in November 2003.

Chapter Four

Settling Down

After several years of touring, Christina Aguilera was forced to cancel a mid-2004 series of performances because of a vocal injury. The series was intended to introduce a new image for the singer. Eventually, Aguilera recovered from her injury and went into the studio to record a new album. At the time, she told *HX* magazine that the days of her bad-girl image were over. "Now the character for this record is 'Baby Jane,'" she told the magazine.

Before the new record was released, Aguilera said to *Time*, "For me, in my heart, I have to move away from [pop]. Even if the label said I had to make another record like that, I don't think I could. Getting older, you just don't want to sing fluffy. You just have more things to say about real life and real people and the bitterness that you get from people."

Aguilera and dancers perform at Madison Square Garden during her Back to Basics tour, which featured her singing, dancing, and changing costumes repeatedly throughout the show.

Back to Basics

Aguilera continued to chart her course and explore her influences with *Back to Basics*, her long-awaited album. In announcing it on her Web site, she described it as a "throwback to the 1920s, '30s and '40s." For the first time, she was credited as the album's executive producer, as she selected several producers in addition to dozens of singers and musicians. "Some of the songs are kept authentic, sticking to a really raw, old-soul sound, where others combine elements of old blues, jazz, and soul with a hard, modern-day edge," she added.

Despite the album being leaked onto the Internet two weeks early, its sales were strong when it was released in America on August 15, 2006, followed by international releases. The double-CD set showcased the older influences, with the second disc being

Producer Linda Perry found working with Christina Aguilera a memorable experience.

recorded live with producer Linda Perry, who also worked with her on *Stripped*. Perry and Aguilera cowrote every song on the live disc. The enhanced video component included a behind-the-scenes mini-documentary on how the album was recorded.

Perry told gossip Web site TMZ.com how they recorded "Beautiful." Perry wrote the single for herself, but she wound up letting Aguilera use it because of how well she sang it. "Christina came to my house for the very first time because at the time I had a studio in my house. And she was very nervous. She was . . . feeling a little insecure and nervous and vulnerable, and she asked me, 'Could you sing me a song to break the ice, to make me feel a little comfortable?' And, of course, that's the song that's closest to my heart, so that's the song I played for her. And she started from across the room and, as the song kept going, she got closer and closer and closer to me. And it was actually very sweet . . . she's like, 'It's perfect for me.' And I was really taken aback by that.

"Christina came down over the next day. I gave her the words . . . And she starts the song. Well, when I heard that take go down, I got goose bumps all over me. And I knew that was my vocal. And for seven months I fought for that vocal. So, that vocal that made it on the record is the scratch vocal, the very, very first time she sang that song."

Aguilera hit the road again in spring 2007 supporting *Back to Basics*. According to reviews, each show featured numerous set and costume changes, in addition to fresh arrangements of songs from her first two albums. In a brisk ninety minutes, Aguilera took her audiences on a tour of her career from pop princess to who she was at age twenty-six.

In December 2006, Aguilera was nominated for two more Grammy Awards: Best Pop Collaboration with Vocals for her "Steppin' Out" duet with Tony Bennett, and Best Female Pop Vocal Performance for "Candyman."

The Price of Fame

When people appear on national television or release a record, they expose themselves to the harsh glare of today's media, and that glare never lets up. With broadcast and cable television channels running nonstop in addition to the Internet, celebrity doings have become a major business. As a result, performers who hit the big time have to accept the intrusion into their private lives as just a part of their line of work.

Ever since Aguilera appeared on the Disney Channel's *The All New Mickey Mouse Club*, her life has been carefully documented.

To promote her albums, she endured constant questioning about her painful childhood. VH1's *Driven* documentary exposed how her peers ridiculed her during her school years.

Every appearance in public seems to be reported by the media, stealing from Aguilera any sense of privacy.

Later, every male she was seen with at a party suddenly became water-cooler fodder as her potential new boyfriend.

The pressure, Aguilera said at the time, got to her as friendships led to betrayals, and she withdrew to work on *Stripped*. People she performed with and even those, like Britney Spears, she grew up with suddenly clashed with her. Every feud became additional material for the insatiable gossip mill.

Weeks after singing alongside Madonna at the 2003 MTV Video Music Awards, Spears and Aguilera exchanged harsh words. A year later, in an effort to put the fight behind her, she diplomatically said, "There is not truth to the rumors that we hate each other. I have no ill feeling for Britney, and vice versa. I am proud of all the achievements she has made in her career; she is a very hard-working person. I have nothing but love for her."

Pink, who sang with Aguilera on "Lady Marmalade," withdrew from cohosting the MTV European Video Music Awards with her, saying Aguilera "would take the fun out of it . . . It's surprising they're having someone like that in charge." In 2006, R&B diva Mariah Carey got into a public feud with Aguilera. In the summer of 2007, media speculation over whether or not Aguilera was pregnant increased until the day it was finally acknowledged that she was pregnant.

Moving Beyond Music

With her international celebrity status assured, Aguilera increasingly supported various charities. Each of them meant something to her personally. Her chief issue was defending animals, both wild and domestic. She also focused on issues that were closer to home, such as giving ongoing support to Pittsburgh's Women's Center & Shelter. Her other causes have included the National Coalition Against Domestic Violence, Refuge UK, Artists Against AIDS, 1736 Family Crisis Center, the National Alliance of Breast Cancer Organizations, and Defenders of Wildlife.

Since 2003, Aguilera has also promoted products from soft drinks to makeup and fashion. Her first major deal was with the Italian label Versace. This was followed soon after by deals with Skechers' footwear and accessories lines. Plus, she launched Simply Christina, a fragrance she helped create, in October 2007.

Given her dramatic career rise, Aguilera met many people and was rumored to be dating most eligible bachelors in the entertainment world during that time. She began seriously dating Jordan Bratman in late 2002. The music executive, three years her senior, proposed on February 11, 2005, and they married on November 19 of that year. The three-day, $2 million celebration took place in California's Napa Valley. The couple requested that wedding gifts be donations to the relief efforts for those hurt by Hurricanes Katrina and Rita, which devastated areas of the Gulf Coast in 2005.

A month after the wedding, she told *Access Hollywood*, "[Aguilera] is definitely my stage name. I am still going by it professionally. But 'Mrs. B' has been the cute thing that my friends like to call me."

In spring 2007, she admitted that the couple likes to keep things casual. She told talk-show host Ellen DeGeneres, "On Sundays, we just do everything in the house, and we're just cozy and laid back. We don't need to go anywhere. We're just with each other."

Having a Baby

During the summer of 2007, paparazzi began noting that Aguilera's belly was bulging, and gossip columns and publications speculated that she was pregnant with the couple's first child. Both Aguilera and Bratman denied it for months. But when Aguilera canceled a concert tour, that only fueled speculation. Finally, her father admitted it to one journalist. Then in September 2007, her friend Paris Hilton publicly congratulated the couple at the

MTV Video Music Awards after-party, confirming what had long been suspected.

Aguilera and her husband sold their Hollywood Hills home for $7 million that summer, and they bought the Beverly Hills mansion that was formerly occupied by Ozzy and Sharon Osbourne.

In 2008, Aguilera became a mother for the first time. She gave birth to son Max on January 12. That year, she also had her name added to the Hollywood Walk of Fame. She announced a desire to do a tour of smaller, intimate jazz clubs, although motherhood may change the timing.

She told *Transworld News* in the summer of 2007 that she was beginning to read scripts to try to begin a second career as an actress. "It is something that, when I attempt to do it, I want to do it right. So, it's important for

Aguilera and her husband, Jordan Bratman, pose at a party in August 2006. Much as she dislikes the media intruding into her life, Aguilera knows how to play for the camera.

The Baby's Media Coverage

Paparazzi from around the world have made a science out of women's figures, trying to determine who might have had cosmetic surgery or eaten too many sweets or, just maybe, who might be pregnant. All through the summer and fall of 2007, few stories captivated celebrity Web sites and gossip shows more than Christina Aguilera's possible pregnancy.

For months, Aguilera refused to acknowledge a pregnancy one way or the other. Even after friends and relatives blurted the news, she obviously wanted to keep it secret. Additionally, she continued to wear tight clothing, so her abdominal swelling was viewed with great interest.

All during this period, she continued to project an image of a woman in love, trying to make music and enjoy time with her husband, Jordan Bratman.

It wasn't until November 2007 that Aguilera finally admitted what everyone clearly concluded on their own. Some time earlier, she was interviewed by *Glamour* magazine, and when she was asked about her New Year's resolution, she said, "That'll be about the time I enter into mommyhood, so I'm hoping to have started a beautiful family with my husband!" When the issue was about to go on sale, the quote was released to the public and the speculation shifted to what the baby's gender and name might be. It was the December 2007 issue of *Marie Claire* that carried the news that the baby was a boy. Max Liron Bratman was born on January 12, 2008.

In 2007, Aguilera and her husband bought this Beverly Hills mansion, which was formerly owned by Ozzy and Sharon Osbourne. The home was featured on the Osbournes' hit reality TV show.

me that I do choose the right first role for myself. I am looking forward to moving into another form of what I feel is another creative outlet for me, and that would be acting."

Additionally, Aguilera was already assembling material for another album. She promised it would be "completely different . . . We're going to keep it short and sweet."

Timeline

December 18, 1980 Christina Maria Aguilera is born in Staten Island, New York.

March 15, 1990 She appears on *Star Search*, a televised talent competition, but she loses the competition.

Fall 1993 She joins the cast of the Disney Channel's *The All New Mickey Mouse Club*.

1998 She records demos that lead to her being signed to record "Reflection" for Disney's *Mulan* movie soundtrack; signs a recording deal with RCA Records in the same week.

August 24, 1999 *Christina Aguilera*, her first album, is released.

September 12, 2000 *Mi Reflejo*, her Latin album, is released.

October 24, 2000 *My Kind of Christmas*, a holiday album, is released.

October 29, 2002 *Stripped*, her second major album, is released.

February 11, 2005 Boyfriend Jordan Bratman proposes.

November 19, 2005 Bratman and Aguilera marry in Napa Valley, California.

August 15, 2006 *Back to Basics* is released in America.

January 12, 2008 Son Max is born.

Discography

Albums

1999 *Christina Aguilera*
2000 *Mi Reflejo*
2000 *My Kind of Christmas*
2001 *Just Be Free*
2002 *Stripped*
2006 *Back to Basics*

Studio Singles

"Genie in a Bottle"
"What a Girl Wants"
"I Turn to You"
"Come on Over Baby"
"Dirrty"
"Beautiful"
"Fighter"
"Can't Hold Us Down"
"The Voice Within"

"Ain't No Other Man"
"Hurt"
"Candyman"
"Slow Down Baby"
"Oh Mother"

Other Singles

"Reflection"
"The Christmas Song"
"Pero Me Acuerdo de Ti"
"Christmas Time"
"Nobody Wants to Be Lonely"
"Falsas Esperanzas"
"Lady Marmalade"
"Infatuation"
"Car Wash"
"Tilt Ya Head Back"
"Hello"
"Tell Me"

Glossary

cover song A new version of a song that was already established in the minds of mass audiences when it first was performed by another musical artist.

demo A rough audition recording to "demonstrate" how a person sings or a band sounds. These are used to encourage record labels to sign them as new recording artists.

diva A term for a distinguished female singer usually related to opera, but it has been extended to describe the prima donna behavior of some popular performers.

manager A person hired to handle the business side of a performer's career, from negotiating recording contracts to arranging concert tours and ensuring the performer's career is on an agreeable trajectory.

platinum album A measure from the Recording Industry Association of America signifying one million copies of a single work have been sold.

producer A person responsible for the particular sound of a recording; he or she arranges the musical instruments, voices, and other sound effects to complete a piece of music.

For More Information

Grammy Awards

The Recording Academy

3402 Pico Boulevard

Santa Monica, CA 90405

(310) 392-3777

Web site: http://www.
grammy.com

The organization that issues the
Grammies, one of the most
prestigious awards in music.

MTV

1515 Broadway

New York, NY 10017

Web site: http://www.mtv.com

Cable channel featuring music
and music-related program-
ming. Pop culture authority
and designator of the MTV
Music Video Awards.

RCA Records

1540 Broadway

New York, NY 10036

Web site: http://www.
rcarecords.com

One of the top recording
companies in the industry.

Web Sites

Due to the changing nature of
Internet links, Rosen Publishing
has developed an online list of
Web sites related to the subject
of this book. This site is
updated regularly. Please use
this link to access the list:

http://www.rosenlinks.com/
cmtm/chag

For Further Reading

Bianco, David P. *Parents Aren't Supposed to Like It: Rock & Other Pop Musicians of the 1990s*. Farmington Hills, MI: U·X·L, 1998.

Cooper, Kim, and David Smay, eds. *Bubblegum Music Is the Naked Truth: The Dark History of Prepubescent Pop, from the Banana Splits to Britney Spears*. Los Angeles, CA: Feral House, 2001.

Dimery, Robert, ed. *1001 Albums You Must Hear Before You Die*. New York, NY: Universe, 2006.

Dominguez, Pier. *Christina Aguilera: A Star Is Made—The Unauthorized Biography*. Phoenix, AZ: Amber Books, 2003.

Hal Leonard Corporation. *Selections from MTV's 100 Greatest Pop Songs* (MTV Music Television). Milwaukee, WI: Hal Leonard Corporation, 2006.

Whitburn, Joel. *Joel Whitburn Presents a Century of Pop Music: Year-by-Year Top 40 Rankings of the Songs & Artists That Shaped a Century*. Menomonee Falls, WI: Record Research, 1999.

Bibliography

Davidson, Jeff. "How Christina Stumbled into 'Beautiful.'"
TMZ.com. Retrieved August 25, 2007 (http://www.tmz.com/
2006/07/18/how-christina-stumbled-into-beautiful).

Scaggs, Austin. "Dirty Girl Grows Up." *Rolling Stone*. Retrieved
August 25, 2007 (http://www.rollingstone.com/news/story/
11111757/christina_aguilera_still_dirty_after_all_these_years).

Silverman, Stephen M. "MTV Host Aguilera Disses Media
'Rubbish.'" *People*. Retrieved September 10, 2007
(http://www.people.com/people/article/0,,626980,00.html).

VH1. "Driven." Retrieved September 6, 2007 http://www.
vh1.com/shows/dyn/driven/60088/episode_about.jhtml).

Walters, Barry. "Live Review: Christina Aguilera's Back to Basics
Tour." *Rolling Stone*. Retrieved August 25, 2007 (http://www.
rollingstone.com/news/story/13881015/live_review_christina_
aguileras_back_to_basics_tour).

Index

About the Author

Robert Greenberger is a writer and journalist who, for nearly thirty years, has covered popular culture and the people involved with entertainment. His work has appeared in *Rockbill*, *Heavy Metal*, *Starlog*, *Headliner*, *Worlds of If*, *Video Games*, *Sci-Fi Universe*, and *Comic Book Artist*, and on the Sci-Fi Channel. He continues to cover the genre for the Web site ComicMix (www.comicmix.com). Greenberger makes his home in Connecticut.

Photo Credits

Designer: Gene Mollica; **Editor:** Nicholas Croce
Photo Researcher: Amy Feinberg

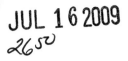
JUL 1 6 2009
2650